C000097712

<u>The Self-Harming Pacifist</u>

An admission about depression, musings by Zac Thraves

INTRODUCTION

First, I would like to state clearly that I am not a doctor, psychologist or behavioural expert. I am a qualified mindfulness practitioner and I am diagnosed with depression. This book is personal experience about how I have learned to cope with the condition of my mind.

I liken depression to a condition; some prefer an illness. I see it now as a part of me that makes me who I am. During this book I will try to explain what I went through and how it feels, it may be different for you and please only take my words as my experience, not as a tested formula for a way forward. However, if it has worked for me, then I don't see any reason why it should not work for others.

The Self-Harming Pacifist started out as a script way back in 2008 when I was in a severe and dark depressive state that lasted years, culminating in a complete breakdown in 2015. It was bouncing off that that I discovered mindfulness and then I saw a light, a tiny spark, that has led me to ditch the tablets and recover myself fully. I still have depression; I know there is no cure for the soul. Yet I am happy with who I am thanks to meditation and a mindful approach to my world.

The script was abandoned; it was a good script about a young man covered in scars who charts his way to France and finds love. His scars were his story, and each one was a memory. I have harmed myself and I have the scars to show for it; they are a reminder as to how fragile I am, and rather then see my scars as something to be ashamed of, I shift that and see them as a reminder of how strong I am and how far I have come. The feeling never goes away, it is like grieving; the emotion is there, it just moves a little further away. But it hovers, in the background, in the whisper of the trees.

Welcome to my journey, and to me, a self-harming pacifist.

PART ONE

'It's too bad she won't live. But then again, who does?' *Gaff, from Blade Runner, written by Hampton Fancher and David Peoples.*

Sometimes when I wake, it feels as if I have been spending the night staring at Edward Munch's The Scream.

That hollowed, howling mouth seeping into your sight like a spitting black hole and wrapping itself around your soul, making it impossible to weep or to fight. I lie lying there like a great fat bear after supper, limbs as lifeless as a body in a morgue, waiting for the inevitable; for the hands of the figure to place their chilled bones around my neck and grip tight. Then, for those dark eyes to bore into my soul and offer me a choice:

Today do you wake and live, or do you decide on another option?

Options include, but are not limited to:

- Sit and sulk
- Prepare a ritualistic sacrifice of one's own life
- Lie in bed for as long as is needed for my body to waste away
- Beat myself with the stick of guilt and judgement
- Get up, damn it get up!

This is not an everyday occurrence, but a regular one. I dream of vicious puppets (oh how I would long to see a puppet appear in the guise of Sooty and Sweep, or the Tracy Brothers, perhaps even Captain Scarlet), these over-bearing, hideous creatures have warped faces as if they have been stamped on by a steel-toe capped boot and then left to rot in an unwanted attic. They appear from the dark corners, the shadowed recesses, from behind splintered wooden doors.

The mind is adept at playing games with the emotions, and often winning.

Which is why I choose to write this story, my journey, through the gates of hell and across the river Styx; and I often ask myself, what if this journey we take into the darkness is what being a human is all about?

I read an interesting tweet about committing suicide by the writer Matt Haig and the very idea of committing to suicide. He argued that you commit to life, you commit to a person or people, you commit to a career and to your dreams; suicide is not a commitment but a terrible outcome of an illness. I wonder if this word for it is born of the days when you were committed to an insane asylum because society neither had the need nor the patience to deal with you? The old time thinking of locking the difficult away still lingers in our modern world like a ghost whispering in the backs of the minds of those who don't suffer such emotions, leading to the stigma, born of fear, that emanates around the globe. Echoes of those screams sit in the paintings of Munch and the like, and filter into our subconscious. We who listen are the ghost-carriers, the portals to the other dimension.

We are all connected.

I'll Be Right Here

Exhibit A)

A completely made up theory/equation:

E.T. is us as much as we are Eliot

That is why the story of Steven Spielberg's E.T. The Extra Terrestrial affects us so emotionally. It marks both the beginning and the end of our journey through childhood and into adulthood; or, for childhood read imagination and for adulthood read reality. E.T. is our higher plane, our fantasy, our imagination; Eliot believes in him and as he steps into the wider world, of school, exams, college and work, he must wave goodbye to all of that and focus on reality. The reality of growing up cause's acne and aching limbs. Well, maybe that is just part of growing up.

As E.T. points to his heart and utters, "I'll be right here." He is telling all of us that we find our truth and ourselves within and inside us. We are our hearts and our imaginations, our dreams and our desires.

Don't bury those treasures too deep, mark an X on your map, because when you wake from this listless pattern of working and sleeping, you may need to lean on your own E.T. in order to re-stabilise.

Exhibit B)

Another made-up theory that may be easy to remember:

Phone Home occasionally (home = you)

There are ways of bringing you back home and turning your gaze once more to the stars and to the endless possibilities of your life.

Let's Talk about Depression

For me to cope with the debilitating fatigue of depression I have stumbled upon various exercises, which have taken years to figure out. My ideas are based on my experience and nothing more. Therefore, please take the following as my own experience, I am not telling you not to do something if you have been advised to do it.

Let's get one thing out of the way, anti-depressants.

If I go the to the surgery and say I am feeling depressed I will be prescribed Citalopram or the like.

If I go to the surgery and say I am feeling low the same will happen.

If I go to the surgery and say I am feeling anxious, nervous, stressed or out of sorts, the same will happen.

All these symptoms are different and, in my view, need to be treated as individually as they appear, yet the same response is given for each one.

When I was on a large dose of Citalopram, I soon found out that I was half a person. The emotion had been eradicated, extracted from me; while I could enjoy a sitcom, I could not laugh at it just as equally as I could not cry because the world was an appalling place. I hated that feeling, I disliked more than the depression the idea that I could not laugh at anything. I was enjoying something, and I could not show it. Therefore, I decided after a long time on the pills that I wanted all of me to be back and in order to do that, I had to accept the bad stuff as well as the good stuff. It was the study of mindfulness that gave me sense. I soon figured out that what I have is a condition which can be lived with, but I cannot live with it when I am half the person.

This is from experience, and I sincerely do understand that these medicines do have a benefit of giving you and your loved ones a break from the pain; but I honestly think that they are not a cure, and that they are handed out too freely. That is what fears me the most about these tablets – painted as a cure, as an answer – given out to whoever needs them.

Why? Anti-d's can work in the short term, but they are just an interim. An interim of inconsequence.

The cure can be within you, but if you remove half of you, the other half is affected.

Wake up, it's a beautiful morning!

A morning routine for me which now works: (I threw away my Citalopram on 4th September 2018).

Wake – ease into the light; shake off the bad dreams, the mares, it's not real, but marvel at your imagination. Woah that was a ride worthy of a great movie. Think about what you want to do today, the good stuff, the exciting things.

Drink - tea, or something that you like to drink, I gave up caffeine and have never wanted it since.

Read – preferably a book. I go for non-fiction in the morning and fiction in the evening. There are some wonderful things you can learn from autobiographies, business books, how companies started, that sort of stuff.

**It is important for people with high levels of emotion and who act as sponges to negativity to not watch the news.

That is the most terrible mistake and one that should not start your day.

Imagine beginning each day by being reminded of all the ills of the world-

having delivered on a plate for breakfast the hunger, famine, murder, crime and political betrayal.

Why do we do this to ourselves?

Breakfast television is for sadists.**

It's no bad thing to miss out on what is going on, I mean if it is, you are going to know about it. But every day? All the time? I'd prefer a weekly round-up, and certainly not for breakfast.

So I read a book, sometimes a fictional novel, sometimes a piece of history or a biography; one chapter a day depending on the size, it is so good for me that I wonder why I have not done it in the past.

Half an hour of that along with the cup of tea and I am ready to face the day. I feel I have given myself an intellectual kick up the rear and then I can roam the world remaining half in and half out of my own world. Or, half and half in imagination. Mindfulness reminds me that through being that way I function better and am sharper.

In fact, by learning mindful mediation you can increase your levels of brain activity as well as boost your immune system. Your imagination is hugely powerful and though the above statement about staying half in the imagination may seem dangerous, just consider all those times you have driven somewhere and then cannot remember the journey; that was your subconscious mind taking you on a trip and you got there in one piece. Instinct takes us a long way, imagination powers instinct.

It is important to be the person who you see in your mind's eye; we are too young to die (Jamiroquai). You can fight the grip of fear that allows negativity to get the better of you –

If you allow it to be part of the person that you are...

Vincent Van Gogh without his 'demons' would not have produced the wonderful images that he did, he is now 'labelled' as a genius, a master of expressionism; in his day he didn't know that and even if he did would it have made any difference?

I think no, and I know that all of us have that same level of genius in us if we learn to accept the WHOLE of us, that includes our 'demons'.

Those monsters – voices – ideas – images – predictions – laments – dragons – burns – marks

Are essential parts of our being

They are how the universe created us

They are our essence

They give us the profound way we see the world

The voices in your mind are not the problem

(Society is)

TRACK TWO…..PARADISE

Challenge: Try to picture your paradise.

When we say the word paradise I would place any money that the first thing to come to mind would be a beautiful green land complete with birds singing and a brilliant cerulean sky draping over the landscape and dissipating into the horizon; the air is full to the brim with peace and tranquillity, hey, there's Adam and Eve with nothing on, woah, it is like Eden.

I didn't create that imagery, but guess Eden is not too far away from the island home of Robinson Crusoe or Tom Hanks' character in Castaway.

That is not really my paradise, but it is a wide idea of paradise that has been indoctrinated into me through Sunday School and then into school itself, this idea of perfection stemming from the words of

cough

The Bible.

Remember that show from the mid 2000's, Lost? Well, my paradise is not the island from Lost, because if I think of an island like that, I imagine the monsters that raged there and a crashed plane and then a secret network of tunnels underneath, and a polar bear. It doesn't work for me.

So, imagine if you will, your paradise.

<u>My Paradise</u>

Paradise is a beautiful garden scented by herbs and bees busying themselves over lush lavender; music plays in the background, a glorious pick n' mix of movie soundtracks, opera, Mozart, Nirvana. A joining together of John Williams followed by Jamiroquai. The theme to Dances With Wolves leading into Pet Shop Boys. Gilbert & Sullivan operetta giving way to Stevie Wonder.

As the music offers a wide variety of emotions I then turn to sustenance, and in paradise I would have wine because wine is by far one of the most satisfying flavours I have ever had, albeit if it is good wine. A soft white Sauvignon with a hint of citrus; or a deep red Rioja with all the power and passion of a bull.

The garden opens to dear friends, and conversation flows as easy and fun. In the corner of the garden, Gizmo the Mogwai plays with a domestic cat. As the light fades sparkling fires light up and we sit down to a large screen and enjoy a movie; it is neither too hot or cold, it is just right, and the time freezes so that every single aspect can be remembered forever.

The film industry is important to the happiness of the world as are all arts. They are storytellers after all, even though you could be forgiven for thinking of the studios as harsh executives demanding success over creativity, the studios have one goal: MONEY.

Yet for all that, for all the formulas and algorithms that are used to get 'bums on seats' and for all the sequels of past hits, or type-cast actors to pull in the crowds, people generally want a good story which gives them the full force of feeling. We want the highs and the lows to feel satisfied. That is the movie magic. It comes from good storytelling.

Marvel would not work were it not for the conflict and the turmoil balancing the humour and the heroic quips. We can all do heroic quips, many of us do in our daily lives, so then we need to balance ourselves by embracing the conflict as well.

We are the balance to The Force – we are the light and the dark. Luke Skywalker channels his inner rage to injure his father in order to ultimately defeat The Emperor; he channels the dark side and while he does, he sees himself in his father. Unlike his father he can bring himself back, he controls and embraces both sides. His father acknowledges this balance and sees what he needs to do, not through his consuming rage but through love, which was always inside him. Love throws The Emperor down the shaft of the Death Star blowing him into a ball of plasma. (Sorry if this should have had a **spoiler alert**)

That is the balance to The Force which Yoda always speaks about, it is the balance within us.

Enough about movies, all of that was simply to explain that my chosen movie for my paradise would be The Empire Strikes Back, which opens up the storyline of Star Wars to allow the conflict in, and it is a story which reminds us that the light does not win all of the time; that is nothing to be feared.

We would sit and watch, some of my friends would have no idea what the movie was about; the sky would turn a deep dark blue and the stars would open like flowers. We would eat fruit crumble, fresh from the day and ease into a story of humanity beautifully told.

That is my paradise, not complete and always open to change. I may feel the need for sparkling water, or a fresh punnet of strawberries. Sometimes I desire a steak, sometimes I deplore the eating of meat and wish for vegetables.

Variety is the spice of life, as the saying goes; but also, openness and understanding –

Try and create your paradise, explore it and see how it builds; most importantly, listen to you.

Some of us find it hard to even whisper what we want, and there is no reason for that. Listen to yourself and notice what your body and mind are saying, because they need the same things, and that comes from you.

Our minds and bodies want to be in sync and happy – do not be afraid to act on achieving your own paradise and to share it with others. If we are open, we listen, we accept those around us and share our ideas with no fear of judgement. A happier place can be achieved, linking your dark and your light into one beautiful colour which is unique to you. Your true AURA.

Just imagine a place where no one is wrong because no-one is judged; it is just that we all think differently.

That is my idea of true human Earthly paradise.

TRACK THREE....UNTITLED

Cancelled Without Prejudice is a term used in passports by governments all around the world. It's a stamp, slammed into passports when said passport is cancelled before it expires. In a way, your homeland is saying to you that you are no longer considered able to comply with the terms of your country and you are no longer welcome to act as a representative. I have no issue with people having their passports cancelled, that works for me, but what do they think this means, when your own form of identity is described as such?

These are the people voted by us to take care of our home and our services; to negotiate with other countries to ensure peace is maintained and humanity behaves as one for the good of the planet. That's the theory of it anyway, the reality is very different, but I hope what most people living in the world would like.

Can we cancel without prejudice our governments and nominate a visionary to reach out to others?

Here in the UK we have a choice of two – much like the US model; we may have other parties who pop up come the time for an election, yet their power is limited and for the most part of the years of cold wilderness in-between elections these voices seldom get heard. The trouble with the idea of narrowing it down to two is that you end up giving the majority a choice between ok and so-so.

I would like the choice between amazing and wonderful; beautiful and marvellous; exciting and...

[insert your own adjective here]

The UK sits on past glories and lives and breathes history, which means that it is stuck. I really feel living in the UK that, although it is the land where I have been born and raised, I am not part of it. I don't think like Englanders, I don't see England as a shining example for the world. I see it as a backward land living off Industrial Revolution thinking, it has not evolved. History is history, and celebrate that if you want, but it is not relevant to NOW. Borders and migrants are a thing of the past, we live on Earth, this planet is our home. I find arguments over controls and passport colours and peoples colours entirely banal and petty. Embrace everyone. Britain has a history of inclusion, as much as a history of slavery. Acknowledge and move forward. Welcome everyone in and let's focus our energies on the environment and poverty.

Then they open Parliament and you have men in tights banging a door with a golden gavel from sixteen something or other. That's not forward thinking, that's up its own arse.

And all of that affects my mental wellbeing. Anxiety is on the rise alongside hatred and separatism.

<u>Musical Interlude</u>

I have a few words for those of you who may be living with anxiety and depression:

You could have a steam train if you just laid down your tracks;

You could have an aeroplane flying if you bring your blue sky back;

All you do is call me, I'll be anything you need.

Time

In the living room sits a clock; it lies dormant on the table which holds up a lamp. The seconds that emanate from the small face issue without a care and serve as a timely reminder that soon, death will come.

The face stares out, watching, listening, waiting; gathering information while it smiles playfully at you between the hours of nine and three. The late afternoon and evening turn this face into more of a grimace; reflecting the demons that rise as the blanket of night sweeps over the landscape.

The clock never falters; the pendulum is impenetrable. As the fog rolls in from the ocean, arcing across the coastline of your soul; as your memories sweep across the sea of regret and gather over the space of reality that lies ahead like a long road, the world starts to turn upside down.

The ticking clock can anger and calm at the same time.

TIME.

A healer and a wound.

TIP: Clock Management

If you want to be happy please look at ten to two. If you wish to be sad start this at twenty past eight. Midnight, as midday, offers a phallic symbol which empowers some while destroying others. Six thirty is the ultimate low, don't think about going to 6.30.

The 1980's have become cool again.

In the 1980's it was cool to like the 1950's style and music, like the music of Eddie Cochrane in the Levi's adverts or Muddy Waters, Percy Sledge and all of that. Those ads inspired a love of 50's style, spurred on by school productions of Grease and then record companies began producing compilation albums of soul and blues.

Life comes around and moves in circles, this is both a blessing and a curse.

While is wonderful to see are the things that made and influenced me in my teenage years come back to being cool. This can be bittersweet. Just a thought back to that time and the brain flips through images of the last thirty years which can become over-whelming, melancholic; joyful and lamentable at the same time. As we get older the number of mental images grows, some would call this data-overload.

Youth never belongs to the youth, because it is borrowed from someone else's. Yet, perhaps we should revel in it; because for one moment in our lives those of us who come from the 80's are at a point of being the best source of truthful knowledge for that decade. An imaginary high-five to everyone out there who can lay claim to this and enjoy it, because soon the 90's will be the thing and that is when I lumbered into being some impression of an adult, losing the innocence of life and waking up to the gruesome reality that dreams are not actually the things that others want you to chase after.

Now, twenty years after hitting alcohol to try to keep my dreams alive in my head and block out the harsh grey reality of Britain and its capitalist control of the masses, I have come to the realisa-tion that dreams are the only things that you own; so never let go of them.

You can be an adult in the world and continue to fight for your dreams. Yes, there are people out there who will cry for you to fail, who try to talk you down, who tell you to get a "proper" job (whatever that is, I mean, giving the best part of your life to an organisation who doesn't give a shit about you is supposed to be proper living?). There are always people out there talking you out of doing something because they are too scared to follow the same example.

All I ask is this, what would that ten-year, twelve-year, fifteen-year-old self who still dwells inside you say if you asked? Sometimes looking around with those eyes and seeing where you are is the most scary and eye-opening experience. It can also be a true idea of figuring out what it is that you want from life.

After years of searching and stumbling, years of turning away and trying to forget; years of regrets and missed chances; years of falling into dark pits and trying to claw back out – of being lost in a forest and unable to see the directions...

A conclusion has been reached – born of internal conversations between all of me, from the day I was born to the person staring in the mirror at that moment in time. A simple statement of intent that carries me through the turmoil and struggles that continue to dominate my thoughts and try to wrestle control. An instruction to myself when those demons' surface for air and want to ingratiate themselves back into my world. A way forward for myself when I decide on which way to turn and a mantra that drives me towards chasing the things that I want and need in my life:

I WANT TO BE HAPPY, NOW

TRACK FOUR – THE SELF HARMING SYNDROME

Picture the scene…

A raging sea: a fierce sky sending pellets of rain down onto a beleaguered crew who cling to a vessel splintering to the wind. The waves rise like bulging walls and smash down their vicious foam onto the delicate skin of the hapless sailors. One of whom is intrepid adventurer Ulysses, a man on a mission and here, amidst the battering storm his attentions are being lured by the soulful tune of the deadly Sirens of the sea. They offer peace and calm, beauty and protection; they offer death and they offer suffering while wrapping you in their wicked song.

The legend says that to protect Ulysses from this sensual temptation, he tied himself to the mast in order to prevent him from being lured in by the call of the Sirens.

People with depression must do the same.

A self-harming pacifist is exactly that: someone who enjoys harming the one, but not the many.

Almost as Spock was want to say, "The needs of the many outweigh the needs of the few, or the one."

Does that make self-harmers selfish?

Of course, when one decides to take a knife from a draw, or to punch themselves in the arm or however the chosen method is, the words of Spock are not in the forefront of the mind. They are not even the words of Spock or Leonard Nimoy, but that of a writer, like me, trying to instil some kind of order into a chaotic world.

That Spock's mantra has traversed over fifty years is a testament to the power of the words, and for words in general.

But, the question remains, are self-harmers selfish?

Imagine a kettle of boiling water with no spout for the steam to escape, as the water continues to boil so that pressure within the kettle will increase. As the pressure inside reaches breaking point it explodes, the outcome being extremely violent; the kettle would be destroyed; the landscape around the kettle would be severely damaged, perhaps permanently.

To alleviate the pressure in the kettle, a small hole is inserted, the spout, for the steam to escape.

A small hole is created. Just enough to allow the pressure out.

The kettle is the self-harmer; and what they are doing is performing an entirely saving and selfless act in order to keep harmony and peace in their world.

My Method

In the morning my head would be bulging as if about to burst

Voices echoed around my head, creating an enormous noise

Static on the radio...screaming from a crowd

My eyes watered for no reason

My heart wanted to scream

My brain could find no resolution

Crying was not a powerful enough release

So, you turn to the kitchen utensils and take a long hard look at the largest knife you can see

It gleams in the sun; its cold metal smiles at you

You pick a spot you can cover

An actor contemplating a tattoo

Your emotions flood into the foreground of your world

Every ill you have done suddenly returns

It is the most important thing in the world

You start with a scrape

You plunge the knife a little harder

You draw a small line of blood

You decide to dig deeper

Once finished, the knife is casually washed up as if used to slice a tomato, before it is returned to the draw and then you, the SHP return to whatever it was you had been doing:

reading – writing – watching tv – preparing lunch for your small child – telling those that you love that you are running a bath.

Non-aggressive and non-life-threatening harming could well be a normal thing to do; it is our attitude to it and our fear of the mental condition that stops us from embracing it.

Instead in our world we accept smacking wives and children for being wrong; we accept people in power raping young women; we accept a fight in the street or violent demonstrations; we accept police brutal-

ity; we accept parents scolding and hurting their children, pulling their hair or yanking their arms; we accept that domestic violence occurs and there is nothing that can be done about it; we accept abusive drunks blaming their behaviour on alcohol.

We accept all those ills in our society and yet, if you self-harm, it is seen as a sign that you are crazy, a wacko, a nut-job. Why would you do that? Well, it's far better for me to hurt me that it is for me to hurt someone else, or someone I love. Self-harming does not mean suicide, it means self-harming. Yes, it can lead to suicide, but so can alcohol and nasty comments and mistreatment as a child and abusive relationships.

If I had instead gone to smack someone in the head to release the pressure and pummelled their brains into the pavement I would have been arrested and possibly imprisoned and told not to do it again. That is not acceptable behaviour.

But at least people would have understood that type of behaviour, so they would have no need to cross the street when they saw me coming towards them because I'm a sick self-harmer.

Is that a society we should accept?

The institutions and hospitals that were used to house the 'crazies' are reminiscent of Ulysses being tied to the mast of his ship. His idea of the Sirens being all powerful is the same kind of thinking that the 'sane' among us have of the people classed as mental-health sufferers. In order to stop them from hurting themselves and us we must lock them up, tie them up, chain them up, remove them from the temptations of the underworld while their brains fry with thoughts of being utterly mad. (Literally brains were fried with electro-therapy)

The solution, I believe, is to get to a place where you can be the full you, all internal straight-jacket and all, and be free to roam as one of the "normal" ones. If Ulysses had an ounce of self-control, perhaps those pesky Sirens would not have been able to seduce him into their waters and devour him with sex.

Men, we are still led to believe, are unable to control any of their emotions, and women are the evil ones trying to gain power on the back of that.

What self-harmers are trying to do is what they can in order to give themselves a chance at life; it may not be seen as a logical way of dealing with a problem, but then we are not dealing with an algorithm or an equation, we are dealing with emotion, the most powerful tool we have in our arsenal. Rather than seeing people with serious mental health problems as "a problem", by talking and acknowledging, there is a way to embrace the power that we have within us in order to create a life accepting those emotions. They are as real as the pain you receive when you fall over, but sometimes when you fall you don't need a plaster or a trip to the hospital, you just need to sit and regather your thoughts and regain your focus. The pain will subside, as does all pain; our bodies are very good at looking after things; so, we should also trust our brain to do the right thing too. There are techniques out there that have been used for centuries to balance our emotions, to accept our personalities and that we are all different. Mindfulness, meditation, calm and stillness. Ideas that have been used and proven to help with the symptoms of anxiety and depression.

Here's my idea: perhaps the people who self-harm are the strongest, and have a more rounded understanding of the world, their world, and the answers that lay somewhere in between.

TRACK FIVE…
LABYRINTH

The minotaur lurks the dark avenues of Co-Op.

a bursting kaleidoscope store – faces

glare from packets, eating your wallet –

penetrating the soul, flirting

and luring you into their trap.

People at every turn

Standing – reading – watching

Learning – contemplating

And you, struggling to gather

Enough fight to move past them.

The corridors shrink

Deeper you wander

Food turns to cardboard

Tins turn to bottled glass

Collapsing on the floor

Unable to breath, unwilling

To gather the groceries

The minotaur wins and you

Exit bag-less

Do you dare enter the Co-Op labyrinth?

TRACK SIX: TOXICITY

There is a gateway to being alive and you hold the key; don't try to recreate the past, focus only on the now; on your dreams and your map to make them come true.

Regrets are pointless, they are just like sitting through a television show that you hate. The only reason you tune into that channel of regret is because it is about you. If you give it credence you give it power. Just like we do to toxic people in our life, and we all have those even if we don't quite know who they are.

I remember some, and when I think of those people, I can only say that I am regretting. I regret that I behaved in a way that made them feel good when it was not reciprocated, and that I let them get away with it. I regret that it has taken me years to recognise that this is what they did to me. So, you see, regrets are pointless, because ultimately you have to ask:

WHAT DOES IT MATTER NOW?!

The answer is that it doesn't, because if I had decided to do something about it that would take up time where I could be doing something far more productive and the result would be what? A small sweet victory quickly forgotten. a massage of the ego? Ergo, what is the point, please try to always move onwards and upwards towards something greater than you did yesterday. Never mull over the past.

Toxic people lurk everywhere, like the Minotaur or the Medusa.

They appear as a friend, like a Syren and quickly wrap their slices of negativity and evil over your veil giving you blurred vision. These people are sometimes referred to as 'energy vampires' simply because they suck away all the good energy that you have been storing up to fight your own battles and then drain you of that resource. These people usually come in the guise of someone who asks you how you are and then you see their eyes glaze over as you speak, before they quickly change to subject to tell you all about them.

Toxic people behave in the sly way where they are your friend in your company and do a swift U-turn when you are away. You know they are toxic by the very simple act that you hear from someone else their opinion of you. The difference between a toxic friend and a true friend is that you will not hear such things, because when you meet a person who likes you for being YOU, they just want to be in your company and don't give a thought to changing your thinking or convincing you to change your opinion to match theirs; they will not walk away in an argument because you are having what adults call, a discussion; they will not allow the phone to go cold for a long period of time and only call you when they need something; they will offer to help you even if it disturbs their plans.

The opposite of toxic is harmless, or helpful, or healthy; therefore, seek harmless friends.

Harmless people do not manipulate, they will compromise. There is one wish that a harmless friend has when they are in your company, to see you smile.

Those types of people don't turn their back on you, regardless of what you may or may not have done. They offer a hand, and they know you will take it. They notice when you are in need and they step forward. They are not driven by others but by their own convictions. Likewise, you reciprocate because being a friend is a two-way street. If you go through the types of emotions that I go through you would understand the importance of trust, of honesty and of openness. When you are a self-harming pacifist, no subject is off limits; everything needs to be explored in order to find an understanding. There is no right or wrong.

If, like me, there are complications with your emotions, toxic friends only wish to see you when you are UP. That is a good indication that they are not the type of person who will stick with you when the shit hits the fan. They may not understand what it is that you are going through, and I have friends who have no idea of the emotion that I go through when I am feeling down; but they are aware that it is not for them to understand, it is only for them to offer a hand and support.

I guess that in this world, or in our current society born of the idea that greed is good, toxic is a more powerful word than harmless. I mean, harmless means safe right and who wants safe?

Well, in reality, we all do.

When the curtains are closed and the storm rages; when the lines are cut and lights go dark; when the wind howls and the glass shatters; when you are alone and don't know where to turn; when the bitter ice nips at your toes and you can't shrink away enough; when the ones you think you can trust betray you. That is when you know who you can turn to.

Everyone needs safe, whether we recognise it or not. Safe. Harmless. Healthy. Helpful. It's in the Thesaurus.

Positive words that contain far more energy and power than they appear. When you say them out loud you feel so much better.

TRACK SEVEN: NUMBERS AND MUSIC

Numbers play an important role in the universe, just ask Einstein. The universe is made up of mathematical equations which go way over my head and completely bamboozle me. Yet my life is driven by numbers, I think it might be the way my brain is wired. My main source of numerical aid is the number 28. This has appeared throughout my life for as long as I can remember and could mean anything. It could be my guardian angel keeping an eye on me; it could be the rule of attraction and I see it because I want to see it. Yet there is a belief that numbers play role in our experience with the world, so this chapter is all about numbers that I believe in and that I think add some character to the person that I am.

Here goes...

Seven is an important number.

Here's a trick I did in real time while writing this piece: go to a favourite movie and glance through the scene selection on the DVD, find an important number in your life and go to that scene.

I have just done it and used a very important movie in my life called The Empire Strikes Back. I went to chapter 7 on the disc and it was entitled Obi-Wan's Instructions. What does this mean?

Well, you can make meaning of anything, horoscopes are a prime example; but consider that me going to chapter 7 of that film at that time meant that I needed to heed the advice of a mentor type figure who would tell me the next step to take on my journey to writing this book or getting somewhere in life. I think that this is a pretty awesome trick.

Let's continue to explore some important numbers in my life in relation to important items that I have, and also let you know why numbers play a large part in thinking.

As I said. the number 28 has a huge meaning for my life, I do believe it is the number of my angel. I really started to notice the number in my life in the latter part of the 1990's. It is my Mother's day of birth as well, so has been with me since my own birth. Since the 90's it has cropped up daily in the kind of way that makes me stop and take note.

Belief in numbers is not a new thing, and Numerology is the idea that numbers shape your character and destiny much in the same way as star signs. I have looked at 28 in the numerology circle and it states that 28 means someone who is a leader and a team worker with some business sense; this is not me. I may be a team worker, but I am not a leader...yet.

Perhaps that will change – I am certainly not equipped with business sense...yet.

So that leads me to think that when I see the number 28, which is daily, I am calmed in the knowledge that my angel is with me. I carry the number on my arm written in tattooed hieroglyphs. It looks like 2 upturned U's and 8 I's.

Perhaps there is a number that you see on many occasions, perhaps you have not noticed. It does no harm to anyone to believe that you have magical numbers and that perhaps it is a form of message from some other dimensional space, whatever space you believe in above or below or around you. It does not make you crazy to believe in numbers, I mean, millions of people believe in an entity they have never seen and who they believe created the world. At least I have witnessed the sight of a number.

7 and 3

These are my go-to numbers when I dare to buy a lottery ticket; these are numbers throughout my whole life that I have liked that kind of work for me. Any footballers I may have enjoyed usually wore the number 7 or 3, players like Maldini or Cantona. In the study and belief of numbers these have a more apparent meaning on my character so do not mean to me that my angel is watching over me, but that these numbers do shape the person that I am inside.

7 is the planet Saturn and means mystery, study and knowledge.

3 is the planet Mars and means talent, versatility and joviality.

When I looked these up, I was surprised to discover that Mars again falls into my life. Being a Scorpio, the power of that planet has driven me along for my whole life. A favourite and safe colour for me is red. The fact that I harm myself probably means there is some violence in my psyche.

It is not a silly idea to find these things out; looking at numbers, or astrology or the like to find out your character is a good way of boosting your own confidence. It can be a method to confirm to you that you are you, it is ok, these thoughts and ideas which shape you, are good. When I see the idea that I have talent, it quietens the voice in my head telling me that I am no good and that voice asking me 'why should I bother?'

I'll give that voice some power now: *This book is a piece of crap idea which no one will give a damn about so what's the point, just get you butt to work and come home and get pissed out of your face, that's what you're good at.*

It can shut up now and I am not going to read the above.

Game time

Find a favourite album and the track relating to your chosen number and see where it takes you.

7

There is a Prince song titled 7, which I love and is on his Symbol album from 1992. Prince is one the biggest musical influences in my life, along with the composer John Williams and The Beatles. I'll also put up there Jerry Goldsmith and John Barry. I find music to be therapeutic and one of our most important forms of communication. One song can say so much more than anything else, and each one of us gets something different emotionally from it. A particular song I like and that helps me meditate is John Barry's Moonraker theme, sung by Shirley Bassey. It sways and moves as if you are floating in space, which I guess is its point. But it does allow my thoughts to glide over your mind with no judgment.

Favourite Albums and the Number 7:

The Cocteau Twins: Heaven or Las Vegas – track 7 is Fotzepolitic

Harry Connick Jr: When Harry Met Sally – track 7 is Autumn in New York

Prince & the Revolution: Parade – track 7 is Venus de Milo

Mozart: Reqiuem – track 7 is Lacrimosa

The Beatles: Abbey Road – track 7 is Here Comes the Sun

Favourite Albums and the Number 3:

Cocteau Twins, Heaven or Las Vegas – track 3 is

Harry Connick Jr, When Harry Met Sally – track 3 is

Prince & the Revolution: Parade – track 3 is I Wonder U

The Beatles: Abbey Road – track 3 is I Want You

Just a few examples and there are a skip-load of albums that I have listened to over the years which only come to mind when you hear them again. If you could catalogue every single tune you have heard, from early classical music to current pop, it would be an enormous collection and extremely diverse. I find that beautiful. I love that an acoustic guitar played by Mark Knopfler on the track Private Investigations is just as wonderful as a choir singing Requiem or Spike Jones & the City Slickers playing silly instruments. It all has a place in the heart, the mind, the soul and in our world.

Take when Paul Simon brought African music to the masses with Graceland and how amazing a track Homeless is. Music is so diverse; it is non-judgmental and opens our souls. When you put a record on, or a CD or stream a track, you do not choose based on any discrimination, you choose because it is something you want to listen to. I hope so anyway, I truly hope that music is a way of ridding our world of racism, sexism and any other ism that deserves no place whatsoever in our lives.

Music is mightily important, and it can lead straight to your heart whether or not you can play an instrument. You do not have to be a connoisseur to enjoy it; you do not need any knowledge of the writer or performer to understand it. When it comes to music you need only do one thing:

Listen.

Through listening you are allowing your mind to calm and re-focus. Play some tracks, close your eyes, open your mind and listen.

Music is accessible to everyone; there are no skills required to hear it. It is probably one of the most beautiful ways we have to communicate.

This book has a Spotify playlist to accompany it, give it a go.

INTERVAL

Please take this moment to try our refreshments,
enjoy a cold drink or visit the public conveniences.
On behalf of the management, thank you.

PART 2

Track 8: Be Kind to You

Do not go out into the wild alone.

There is one thing which is so important to our lives and it happens to be the one thing that we find most difficult to do when struggling to breathe in the waters of depression:

communication...

Just look at that word for a moment and how it is constructed.

'Commun' comes from community and commune, from togetherness and oneness; from all of us sticking together and aiding each other. A family; a bond; a link to what it is to be human, a member of our species. We naturally want to protect, not fight; we strive to be safe, not live in fear.

When that heavy black cloud descends, when it sends forth instructions that you need to be alone and that everyone hates you, or that you are useless and no one can understand, remember that those are lies. Deep-rooted, sadistic, evil lies. This might help, picture a politician telling you those things instead of a voice that you trust and perhaps you can quickly rally against it.

Reach out. We are now living in an age of immediate communication. If you don't want to speak to anyone you have other options:

Text

Tweet

Post

Email

Emoji

They may not be perfect, but they are something, and, as with anything in life, something is better than nothing.

> If you are alone and you feel the signals of suicide or self-harm, please reach out to someone to tell them how you are feeling; we all have someone who will listen, you may think that there is nobody but the honest truth is that there is. How do I know? Because those are the people who say at the funeral that all they had to do was call. Be honest with yourself, recognise the feelings and then be honest with the person you are reaching out to. They may be shocked, scared, unsure, panicked; but they don't want to be sad or grieving for you, being scared is so much easier to overcome. Reaching out starts your journey to getting through it.

There are always going to be times when you need to be alone and just be with you; this is natural, not selfish; people without depression need 'me' time; it's just that when you are diagnosed with depression or anxiety suddenly it becomes strange that you would want to be on your own...almost sinister, because perhaps you are planning your death.

That's not what is happening in most cases.

Sadly, in some cases it is.

But we must be honest about the condition and remove stigma around 'patients' or 'sufferers'. The important thing to do is live your life and sometimes, just sometimes, you can have a lot of fun when you are on your own doing the things that you like to do, when you want to do them. It is liberating and it exercises the imagination. There is no better feeling than that a-ha moment when you decide that instead of being bored, you'll do this! You enter an activity with power and vigour and enthusiasm and suddenly...the day is nearly done.

Let people be people, don't judge others by your own standards or fears or needs. Judgement is all too prevalent in our society, we hear it every day on the television and on the radio and from colleagues and from family. We all have an opinion, it's no wonder some of us have a bad opinion of ourselves. Free yourself, give yourself a break and empty your mind of those negative judgements. Fill your mind with pleasure and fun.

Here's a list of what I get up on my lonely days:

Watch an old movie (child of the 80's, Weird Science is a guilty pleasure)

Listen to music with headphones on

Have a beer in the afternoon with no guilt

Strum the guitar

Make a silly film for Youtube

Write blog ideas

Start a book that I may never finish

Go through old photos

Watch nonsense on Youtube

Sit in the garden (weather permitting)

You get the idea.

Dilegua, o notte!

Tramontate, stelle!

Tramontate, stelle!

All'alba vincero!

Vincero! Vincero!

Track 9: Surrealist Prologue

I'm a dandy highwayman. Fallen into the rabbit-hole and wandering the abyss. Kaleidoscopic colours send me reminiscing; motionless reminders or faces from the past. The future sits in songs, setting alarms to wake when it matters. Unforgiving storms shift weight from one leg to another. We talk, and sometimes say nothing, but it's the eyes that I wish to speak to. Prince Charming may never have existed in the trees, but he lives in the heart. Whether or not he is man or woman, it makes no difference anymore; we exist only for the moment when dreams become truths, myths become stories; hands hold hands.

Don't fear the unknown, the only leap of faith will be in you.

If you see your face in the mirror it means you are real.

Believe in what your eyes are telling you, behind it lies your genius.

TRACK 9: BACK ON TRACK

I have always had an idea that I wanted to be a highwayman exactly like Adam and the Ants.

You know, the 1980's pop star who was a dandy highwayman and a prince charming, if you don't know, check out Youtube for some nostalgic fun.

It is certainly how my subconscious imagines my personae and thus, why I choose to dress in a toned down version of a dandy, I often wear a trilby hat and most often wear a tie with my shirt to work when other colleagues don't bother anymore. I use this as my uniform that reflects a little quirkiness to my character. I only do what I am brave enough to do, yet there is a seed always in my heart that I wish to wear a hint of make-up and painted nails. Perhaps not the smear of white across my cheeks like Mr Adam, but something around the eye and lips to enhance my features.

The reason most of us don't do this, or fear doing this, is because society has made it unusual for a male of the species to go around looking like a made-up dandy, certainly nowadays anyway. We talk about the male and female divide from the women's point of view almost all the time, and rightly so because it is the women who have been made second-class sexual objects since the birth and rise of organised religion. However, there are some men out there crying to the skies for gender equality, and in achieving this to be allowed to express themselves as they wish without also being judged.

I often ask myself why most men that I see here in the town where I live, in Kent behave like a typical bloke while I, in my hat and coat and ties and cravats, stand out as something different?

While I stand out, most men my age blend in with the uniform of tracksuit bottoms and glowing white trainers. So, I'm the odd-ball? Really? I'm not blindly following the crowd and I know who I am. For me the odd ones are those who wish to look exactly like someone else.

This idea that I am odd is another weapon, another stick used to beat me with; when I was a child looking at Adam and wanting to be an anarchist wearing make-up and fancy coats it was exciting and completely achievable. But then something happened: school? Venturing into a larger world? A slow dawning that you are average? The lowering of expectations and putting you safely into the cog of the economy?

Our system seems to spend the first eleven years of someone's life building them up and the next seven years knocking them down. After that you are on your own. Welcome to the world, don't make a fuss, do not pass go and do not collect £200.

Getting older has given me a licence to really be me; I wear what the hell I like and have been known to place some varnish on my nails. I think though that I shouldn't be able to think that what I have done is something radical, I haven't, I've painted my nails. Get over it.

Radical would be painting slogans over bald headed men in track-suit bottoms telling them to wake the hell up!

TRACK TEN

We are now reaching the finale, and I want to discuss what depression is to me and maybe to some of you.

There are various ways that depression manifests, it is extremely serious and can culminate in being taken to a hospital or home, or something they call a recovery centre; for some people that is a good thing and aids their recovery. I am not sure that there are levels of depression, in my mind if you have anxiety or depression it is because you are uniquely tuned to your emotions and that the state of the world around you is not quite right; that world could be you and your family, it could be the government and society, what affects you is up to you and it is only by truly listening to yourself, by meditation, that you are going to find out what that thing is and what affected you. Some science says that what you learn from baby to five will shape your mental character all the way through your life. All those times you have been told **'no, stop, don't, you can't'**, all those phrases stay with you and then, certainly in my case, repeated at school. I have spent thirty years of my life knowing all the things that I can't do. It's time now to turn my energy to all the things I can do. That is what I want for you too. To channel that negative energy that tells you how crap you are into positive energy, trust your imagination to figure out how to make something done, and not listen to those voices reminding you how impossible everything is. Because, anything is possible, whatever that thing is there is always a way to it. Use your energy to, as Captain Jean-Luc Picard might say...MAKE IT SO.

What I am aiming for with this collection of thoughts formulated into some sort of entertainment for your mind is to give reason to minds that are able to complicate things and to help with the idea that these emotions, voices, cries, are YOU.

All of those dark and mysterious thoughts that float through your life make you into the wonderful person that you are, and if you can calm the internal civil war that rages inside, if you can negotiate a peace strategy, if you can give a voice to the dark and to the light, you can be the very person who can achieve anything that you want.

It is harder to be half a person. We need to find balance.

Art, whether that is a painting hanging in a gallery or on your wall; if it is a book carried with you at all times; or a selection of music; perhaps a film or a line from a poem, the use of it as a guide to move you through those dark forests of despair, can greatly help you.

Sometimes the only option is to walk through that forest, there is no way around it; when that is the case you need to arm yourself with everything that binds you to your reality. Your world is unique to you, the way you see things and hear things are only for you. People cannot step inside your head and why should they as they have their own struggles too. This challenge is yours, and when you step from the darkness back into the light you should be proud of yourself, knowing that it can be done; that you have the strength to take you through any challenge that your mind and imagination can offer you.

Art is a form that offers recognition from hundreds of people, that those thoughts and moments that fill you with despair, are not unique to you. Many people suffer and use their gifts to try to help. Art is a wonderful communication source that brings to life what it feels to be alive, all the highs and lows. So why not seek help within the world of art.

Our minds are powerful constructs linked to the wonders of the universe. If you don't believe that then think about where we come from.

We are made from the same molecules that make a star; we are part of the greater universe; we are connected to the planet and to the solar system.

Just like all living things on this Earth.

Everything that harms us is made from minds of mankind. Everything that saves us is made from minds of mankind. Invention is a child of imagination therefore it is important to keep imagining, keep thinking, keep exploring your world and tread down those dark avenues.

If you do, something magical could happen.

Do not fear those dark recesses, fear creates the panic and the confusion; instead, love that you have an idea which could destroy something and then choose not to act on it. Turn it around, find its opposite. With everything that we hate about ourselves, there are things that we love. There must be because everything has an opposite.

We all have a choice. We make choices every second without knowing we are doing it.

Make the choice to live with you, all of you, bring balance to yourself, to your Force, and you can head into the world with everything about you at your disposal. You are your greatest achievement; your life is yours and yours alone. Use the power that dwells within you to make it rich, make it your idea of great. Choose life instead of despair, choose colour instead of darkness.

History of Lunacy

Not very long ago we put people into lunatic asylums. We still lock people away who do not fit into that weird construct we call civilised society. This civilised society is devised by people who deem it civilised to lock human beings away and treat them like the worst kind of animal. Civilised society created zoos to cage animals for entertainment and the idea that being intelligent makes it fine to label and place everything into a box. Everything is labelled, from books to foods to people. The richness of the planet is catalogued; tribal people we don't understand are re-educated into our warped way of thinking so that eventually everyone is the same. Cultures die, history is erased and rewritten. Empire and religion don't like different, everything must be the same. School uniforms; military uniforms; office uniforms. Uniform is key.

Utopia for those in control means we all think the same; we all do the same thing; we all eat the same food; we all watch the same television; we all react the same to situations; we all walk the same line.

Control.

Here are some reasons for being placed into a lunatic asylum way back in the old days, the laws of which are probably still applicable:

Masturbation

Imaginary female trouble

Ill-treatment of husband

Novel reading

Deranged masturbation

Epileptic fits

Excessive sexual abuse

Tobacco and masturbation

Grief

Self-abuse

Women trouble

Suppressed masturbation

Feebleness of intellect

Masturbation for 30 years

There are many more, and the list here is dated from 1864 to 1889.

What is the deal with masturbation?

When we have rules as ridiculous as that, born of religion most likely, then there is perhaps little wonder that people suffer from excruciating anxiety. These rules create the feeling of being boxed in and your instinct is to fight and flee, a basic human instinct.

The only reason for stupid rules such as those is control.

So, if they can't control your mind, they lock you up; they create the idea that you are mad; they pop pills into your mouth to suppress those ideas; they create an epidemic.

They can't control your mind, you can.

You then choose to fit into what we call civilised society, or you do not. The world of imagination is a way to keep your emotions flowing and stay within 'civilised society'. Because the irony of it all is that without people who would be deemed mad, there would be no forward thinking, there would be no new ideas, or invention, art, science or beauty.

Dangerous thinking creates. Creation got us to the moon. Instead of wars, which is another thing we have to thank religion for, we could be heading further out into the universe. The current cycle of those on power is to repeat the same process over and over, getting us nowhere.

That is my thought on it anyway, if you don't agree, great.

TRACK ELEVEN: MY TRUTH

'You cannot learn by forgetting' – Poltergeist 2: The Other Side, 1986

O ver the course of my life I have been to some seriously dark spaces; I have been deep in moments where the only way to freedom was suicide.

I have spent nights so scared of the demons in my mind and the voices in my head that I could not find a safe place to be in my own home. I have sat through days so long they seemed to stretch to eternity, as if time had been put on hold, and then I would watch with panic as the day would crawl into night. As the sun set, my fear would rise with the knowledge that I would have to face all those demons and whispers again.

Mental illness is horrible. It drives thoughts and ideas into your head that make no sense in the light, but perfect sense in the dark.

There was one night that I wandered around my partner's house completely lost; I chased from room to room because I couldn't understand where I was and I was unable to find her; she was in the next room and I couldn't see.

I have bawled my life out to a dog who appeared to patiently listen and sat beside me, her inquisitive eyes looking at me with sadness.

In my own home, I have questioned the existence of people and would believe that I made everyone up from my imagination; that has been one of my most frightening experiences.

It was at a time when I was not working, I could not work; I had split from my wife and my children would come and stay with me for a night and the following morning I would take them to school. My partner would head off to work and I would return home to be alone for the day, in the company of Netflix, music, books, and my own writing.

Yet my brain could only focus on one thing, one painful question: are the people who you said goodbye to earlier actually real?

Once that seed was sown it began to grow; the question would inflate like a balloon. Perhaps they were part of my imagination, after all I am a writer and actor, I create stories and characters and have done since as far back as I could remember.

Why should they be real? What is real? My brain cannot tell between reality and imagination, so perhaps my children are in my mind, perhaps my partner actually does not exist. After all, how can I prove that they do?

I searched through my memories but of course, I could be making those up.

So, I would wander each room checking that things were there, seeing the unmade bed of the children as we hurried out of the door that morning, the plates for breakfast on the kitchen table.

To combat this, I started to leave things lying around. If we played a game the night before I would leave that intact as we left it, not to be touched for days. I would leave my partner's things where she left them, refusing to put them away in preparation for the struggle to come.

I then took a book and I asked my children to write in it, I didn't tell them what to write, but I needed some proof that they were real. I took photos on my phone of stupid stuff, like them eating at the table or sitting on the sofa watching television; I left their pyjamas on the bed until well into the following week. That one question was driving me mad and my mind made it real. It still happens, it is still there, but I now don't give it the power that it had over me. This was around 2013 and my children were both at primary school. Now they are older, and we have better forms of communication.

I was so convinced sometimes that I had made up all these people in my life that I felt like I was going insane. Instead of watching a movie, or relaxing and trying to get better, I would try to piece together all the fragments of memory from the last twelve hours or so and retrace steps taken. You would find me pacing from room to room trying to make the memory solid.

My time off work was not making me better; it was making me worse.

Our minds are powerful instruments; beautiful but deadly. It is amazing in one sense that we can create a world which we feel we can believe in yet at the same time it is immensely scary that we can create a world we feel we can believe in.

<u>Things that helped me through those days:</u>

- **BBC Radio 6 Music**, a wonderful lifeline of great music and wonderful presenters. It helped get my creative juices flowing again.
- **Netflix:** I would watch movies from the 80's, an uplifting decade.
- **Wii:** I would play tennis and sports, try to keep moving and to take my mind off the reality I had created.
- **Walks,** even if it was just to the shops or the local library.
- **Jobs to do;** washing, cleaning, anything to get me going. Earphones in and hoovering was a lifesaver, I discovered Muse and listened to every album.
- **My partner's eyes**
- **My children's laughter**
- **Nature:** sometimes just listening to birds and watching them go from tree to tree is wonderful.

Writing returned to become a thing for me, and I chose to take the path I used to take when my good buddy and I would create stories on cassettes back in the 80's. We would draw up a story, create storyboards for certain scenes, make a movie poster and a coming soon poster. Armed with a cassette recorder, a C90 tape, a record player for background music and our collection of soundtracks, we would perform the story and mostly make it up on the spot.

Back then it was for our own entertainment as there was not a resource to release stories on cassette to a wider audience; the difference now was that I could get the stories out there myself. Be my own publishing house.

It was during those very dark days that I put out **The Sublime Maisie Canon**; I made a trailer for Youtube and published the story on Amazon.

I wrote other stories but have kept them locked away, Maisie was a character I liked, and I felt comfortable sharing her story. She is a strong woman who chases zombies in a hot-air balloon and shooting them with a catapult. I put her out there and she is the only piece of work that I have shared from that dark period of my life.

It is not easy to turn it around; perhaps you don't. Those extreme feelings are still there and sometimes, when my guard is down that question hovers just out of reach. Now I am stronger and have more belief in myself that I can push it aside and get on with my day. Studying mindfulness and practicing meditation has rewarded me with a deeper understanding of my emotions and a more balanced view of the dark thoughts. I have learned that I need the dark and the light if I want to be me. It is important to not dwell too much on the bad stuff and instead live for today. Everyone has angry, sad, or violent thoughts, it does not make you a bad person. Acting on them makes you the villain of your story, not thinking of them.

I could still walk around the house now and wonder if my children are real. They stay now far less than they did, but I see them more often. My imagination could take that avenue if I chose to. But I ask myself, what is the point of that? Instead I focus on when they are next going to be here and what we are going to do. I have accepted that my emotions are mine and I choose to act or not on them. I am in control; this depression is no longer in control of me.

I have combatted many of my demons by regaining focus, and my journey to that started when I attended a workshop called Super Genius, with Ryan Pinnick.

Super Genius is a concept designed for you to achieve your greatness by tapping into your genius. You do this through a form of meditation and discover your real worth. It is accessing your imagination to create and achieve your goals. It works; I was blown away by it and it made perfect sense to someone like me who only focussed on the bad stuff. I began to let that go, I wanted to follow my dreams and I knew that I had it in me to create something special.

From there I moved to meditation and then to mindfulness and I now no longer need anti-depressants or CBT. I am finally at an accepting peace with myself.

I still have depression; I still have days where I want to stop and stay in bed; I still have thoughts of harm and suicide. But now I know what they are, they are thoughts and tomorrow they could be gone. I let them go and that takes away some of their power. Give yourself some time, if you want to lie on your bed do it without guilt. Guilt is one of our worst enemies, just try to get rid of it and be kind to yourself.

I would not be here were it not for my partner, she has saved me on many occasions over the years. She has taught me many lessons, and now I am in the privileged position of being strong enough emotionally and mentally to also help her, guide her, aid her and give her confidence. The knowledge that I can do that, and that I can help my children, has re-focussed my energies away from self-destructing and towards finding solutions.

I know that there is no cure for depression; but I believe that you can learn to live with it. For me it is about maintaining a focus and removing any guilt; keep moving forward and don't worry about the journey. Emotions are emotions, they are good even when they are bad. Live for today.

THE FINAL TRACK

Wonder at the sea; at the easy breathing in and out of the waves; reaching out to you and then falling back, like a nervous love.

Your mind is your library; care for it; carry those memories around with attention, sift through the contents with your precise control. A smell may conjure up a trick of the mind, sit with it for a second or two, acknowledge it and then let it fly away with the clouds and the birds.

Embrace your past; learn from it, it doesn't mean you act on it. We all change as we grow, much like a flower or a tree, don't expect to think the same way in ten years' time as you do now.

Don't expect others to either. People will come and go in your life and this is a part of its richness. You may have friends for life, you may not; it does not matter, what matters is what you are feeling at the time. The promises you make at twenty years old may not feel the same when you are forty; we all have different paths to tread, sometimes they wander far apart from each other. Sometimes they peel away and wind back. That is life.

Life is for living, not for dying. Some people like to live in a bar; some people like to live in a computer; some people love to disappear into books and some people try to make the world a more understanding place; everyone is as much right as they are wrong, so are you.

You are what is most important in your life. Not the dog; not the love; not the teddy bear from when you were four. Not the phone; not the laptop; not the latest argument on Twitter or the latest turn of phrase from some politician.

You.

You pull you through all the time and you must live with yourself all the time – 24/7.

So, when you are alone, take time to be with you; listen to your heart, listen to those voices in your mind. Give you credence and remember that you are doing good. In your life, it is very important that you have days where you can just be you without trying. You can watch that rubbish movie that you love and cry or laugh as much as you like; you can turn your music loud and not worry about others; so you want to stay in bed reading until gone eleven – just do it.

It is important to love you; nobody is perfect, despite what they try to project out there. Everyone has failings and disappointments and weaknesses and fears. Those are the things which make us human, make us believable and make us real.

If you can bind together the dark side and the light, the ying and the yang, you can be the whole that you are looking for.

The illness classed as depression is frightening; it is not something to be taken lightly and should never be reduced to a sound-bite. Thoughts of suicide are extremely scary; living with someone who carries those thoughts and desires is too.

We have become conditioned into thinking that the best way to treat something is to bury it in sedatives to kill the pain. While anti-depressants have a place, they are not a cure. They are not the magic pill which takes it all away, because you are unique.

Treat yourself as such and open your heart to everything that happens with you.

People with depression are for the most part the kindest and warmest people on the planet. They hurt because they feel everything, and we should not be wary of that. The molecules that make up the world which we walk on and the trees which we move through are the same that make us. So why shouldn't we feel something when we witness something that we don't agree with.

For my part, money is not made of the same molecules that make me; the paper is for sure, but money is just an idea. Therefore, the welfare of our forests and our landscape is far more connected to me than an idea of a system that causes so much harm and divide. This means that when I see rainforests being cut down, the seas of the world full of plastic or animals being mistreated, I feel an incredible pull of sadness that can be overwhelming. I don't feel that when I see a company has gone into liquidation.

Perhaps depression is the wrong word. Perhaps emotionally aware is a way forward.

If the world is crying should that not make us sad?

Yet for everything wrong there are enormous things that are right. You can save the world in your way by taking a leap of faith in you. Trust yourself and turn your hand to that crazy thing that you always wanted to do. Belief is your strongest ally.

The things we remember and treasure in history are mainly the works of artists. The bankers and the insurance salesmen tend to get forgotten. Art and science have saved us so far, turn your hand to something great and use that wonderful expanse of emotion to express it. Turn that pain into something greater, use the energy it gives you into something positive. That sorrow and despair, that cry for help and that roar of approval into something that you love.

Living is loving. Remember that. The strength that comes from you when you are feeling depressed can be harnessed and used into something wonderful. Channel that energy and achieve your own greatness.

Epilogue

It is important to note death, because it is the one thing that you can be sure of. When we are born, we are set on a clear path towards death, it is all around us, it is inevitable. Wherever we are we can see it and we can acknowledge it. Yet, we don't like to talk about it and feel ill-prepared when it enters our lives.

Death can be beautiful, like the orange leaves falling from the trees in Autumn. As one door closes another one opens, and if you entered your life fearing that door opening you will always remain in the room where you stand. Life is for living, and death is very much a part of that; it is an important part and one that we should look at when we have those little rows with each other, the disagreements and the insults. Also, when we find ourselves stuck in a place we need to get out of, such as a terrible place of work or in company of people you would choose not to be.

Living in fear is not living; living is living – loving and reaching and achieving and trying, they are all part of living.

So, when your grandparents die or your parents, please don't question the pain; it is the natural cause and effect. You can miss them, you can love them, you can remember them; but do continue to put your feet forward and try to get to where YOU want to be. Each generation pushes on from the last, we all have a part to play in this great story. Don't get stuck by grief, accept it and then move forward. You will never forget them.